Hello!

Hi, my name is Evgeniya Pautova.
I'm a professional free-lance illustrator with over 8 years of experience.

Welcome to my book and thank you for picking it! I hope you enjoy the creative process and have some fun during that.

I tried my best to make the process easier for you - the illustrations are on the single page only so you don't have to color on the spine of the book and also you don't risk to destroy your piece on the other side of the page.

All the phrases and graphics in this book are hand-drawn from scratch by me. I on purpose avoided using any pre-made fonts to make the book even more unique and funky for you.

I believe both work-haters and work-lovers will enjoy coloring these pages and this book will make you smile.

I wish you a happy coloring!
Yours,
Jen

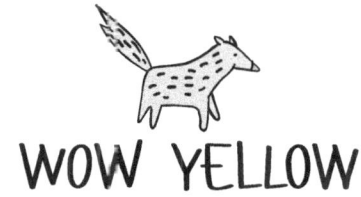

Try your materials

Here you can try your creative mediums or drawing techniques without risking your piece. Just try to feel the material and find the coloring style which suits you the best. Dare to experiment, unleash your creativity and be happy!

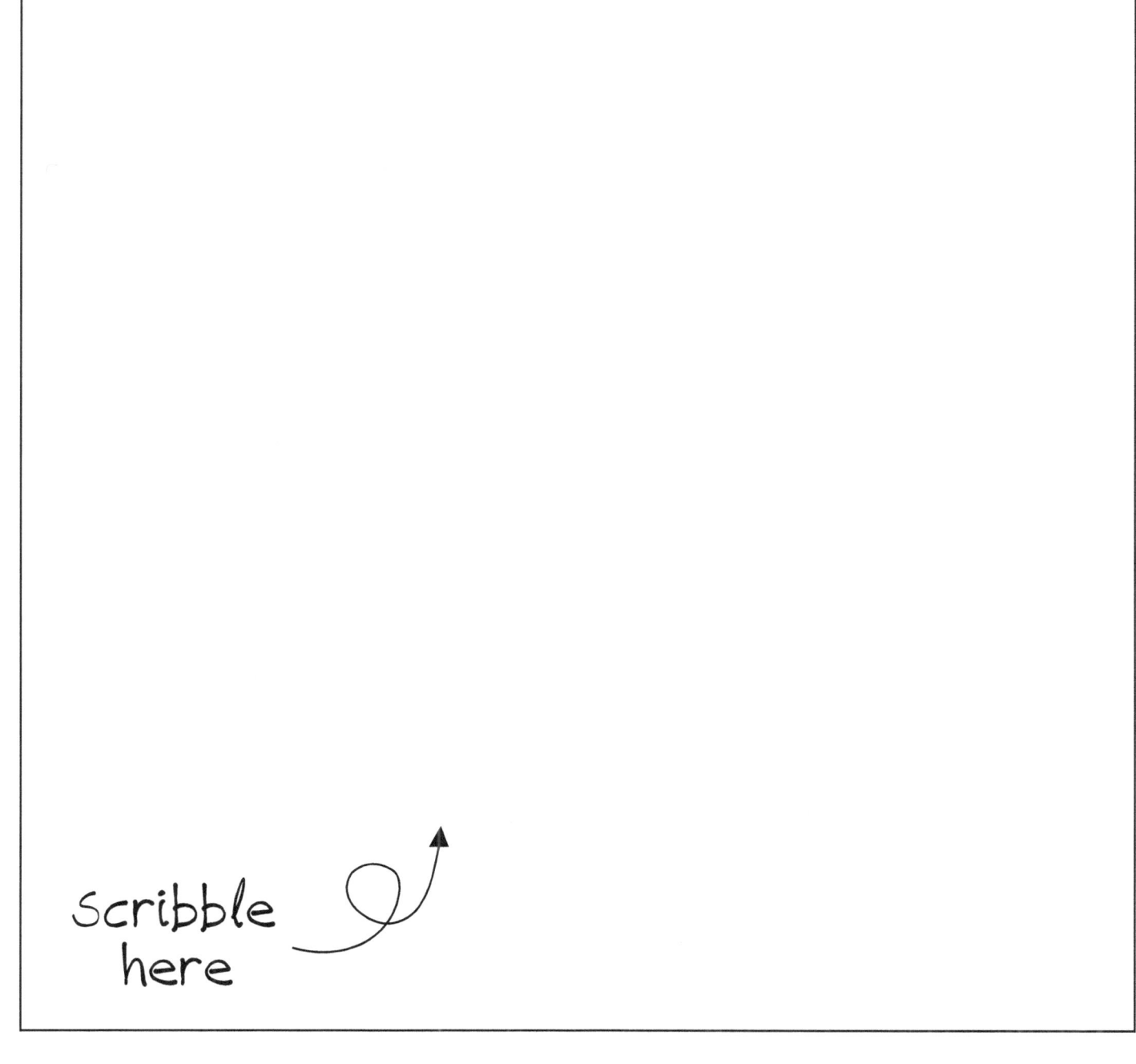

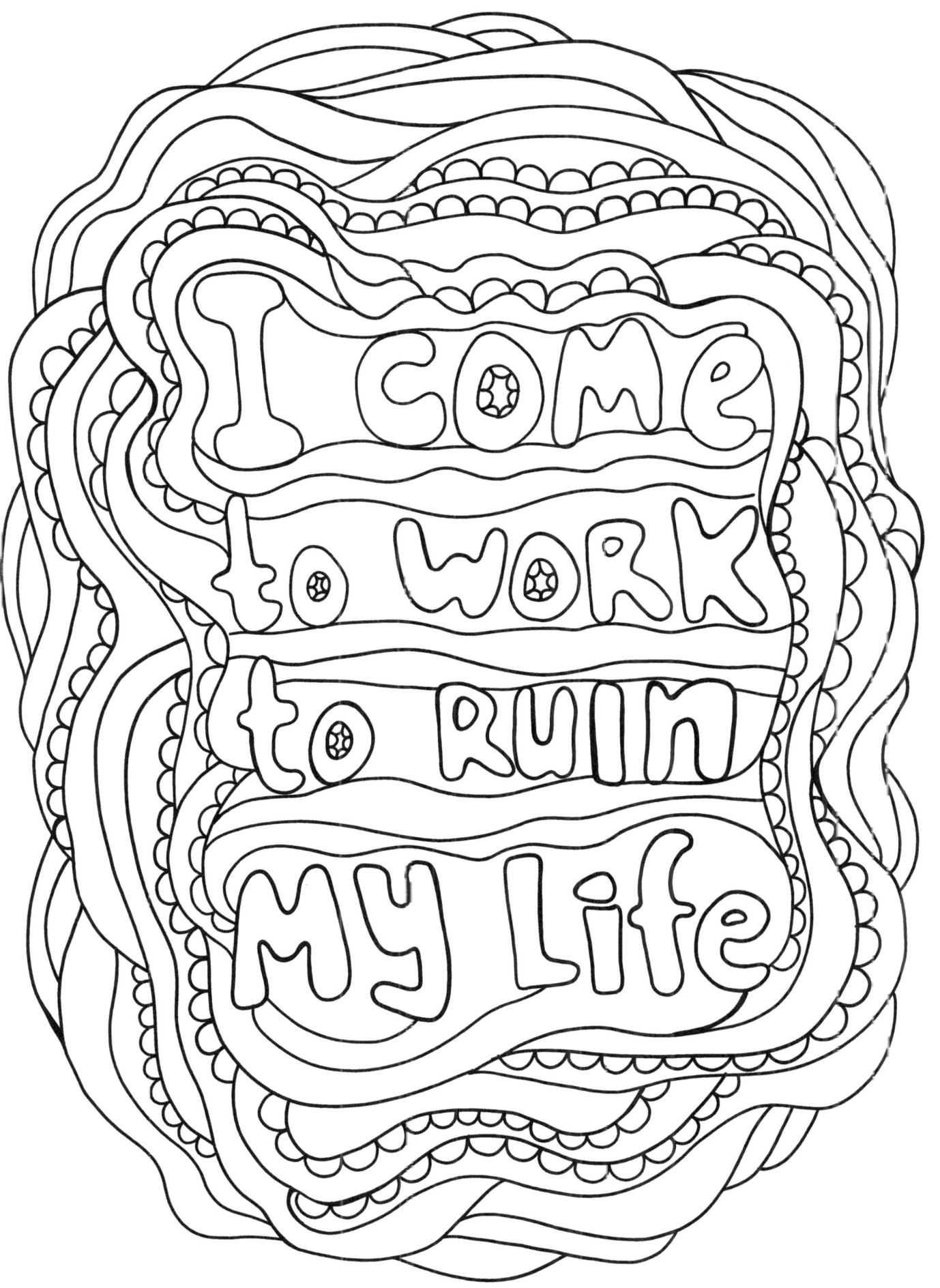

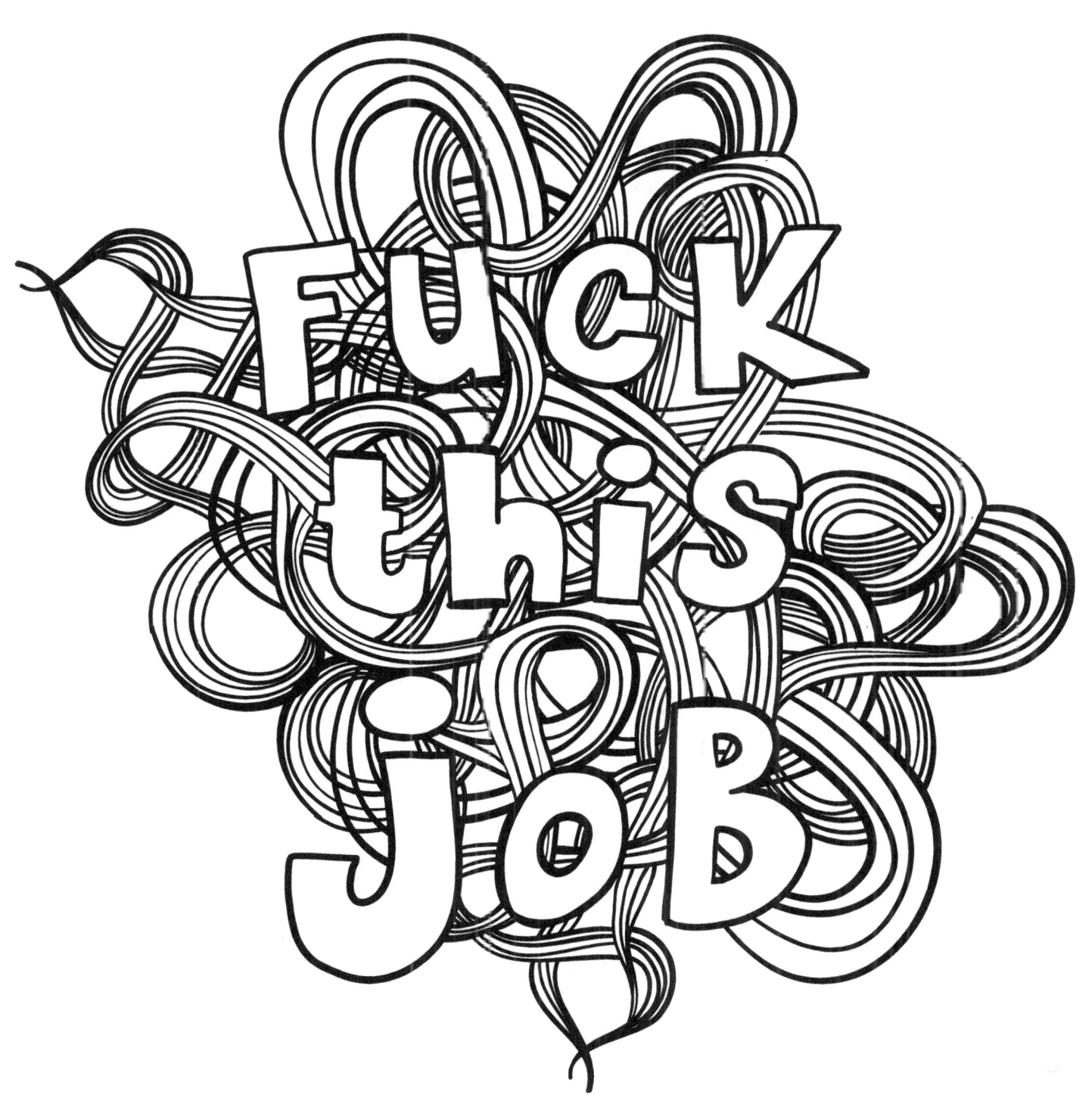

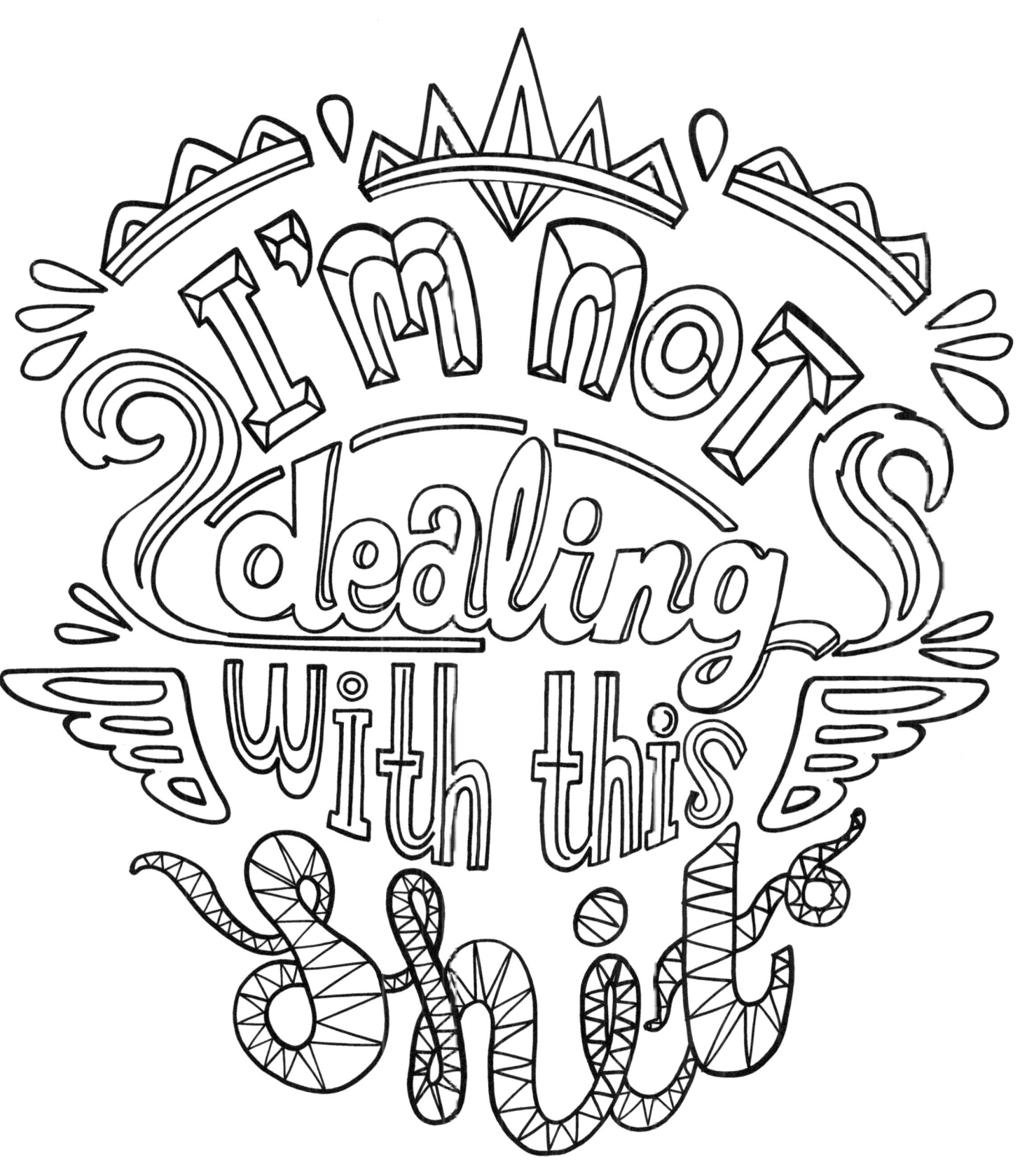

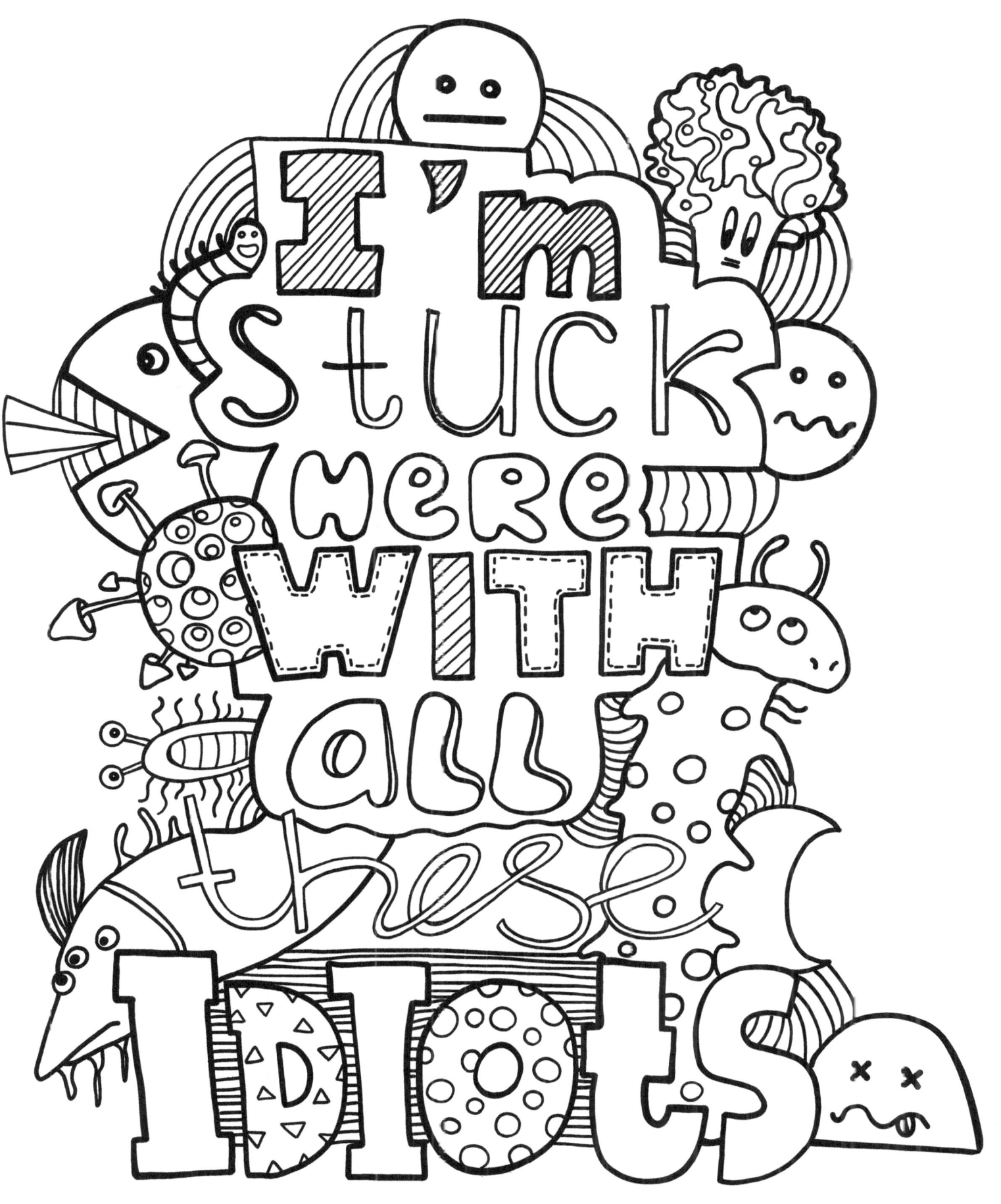

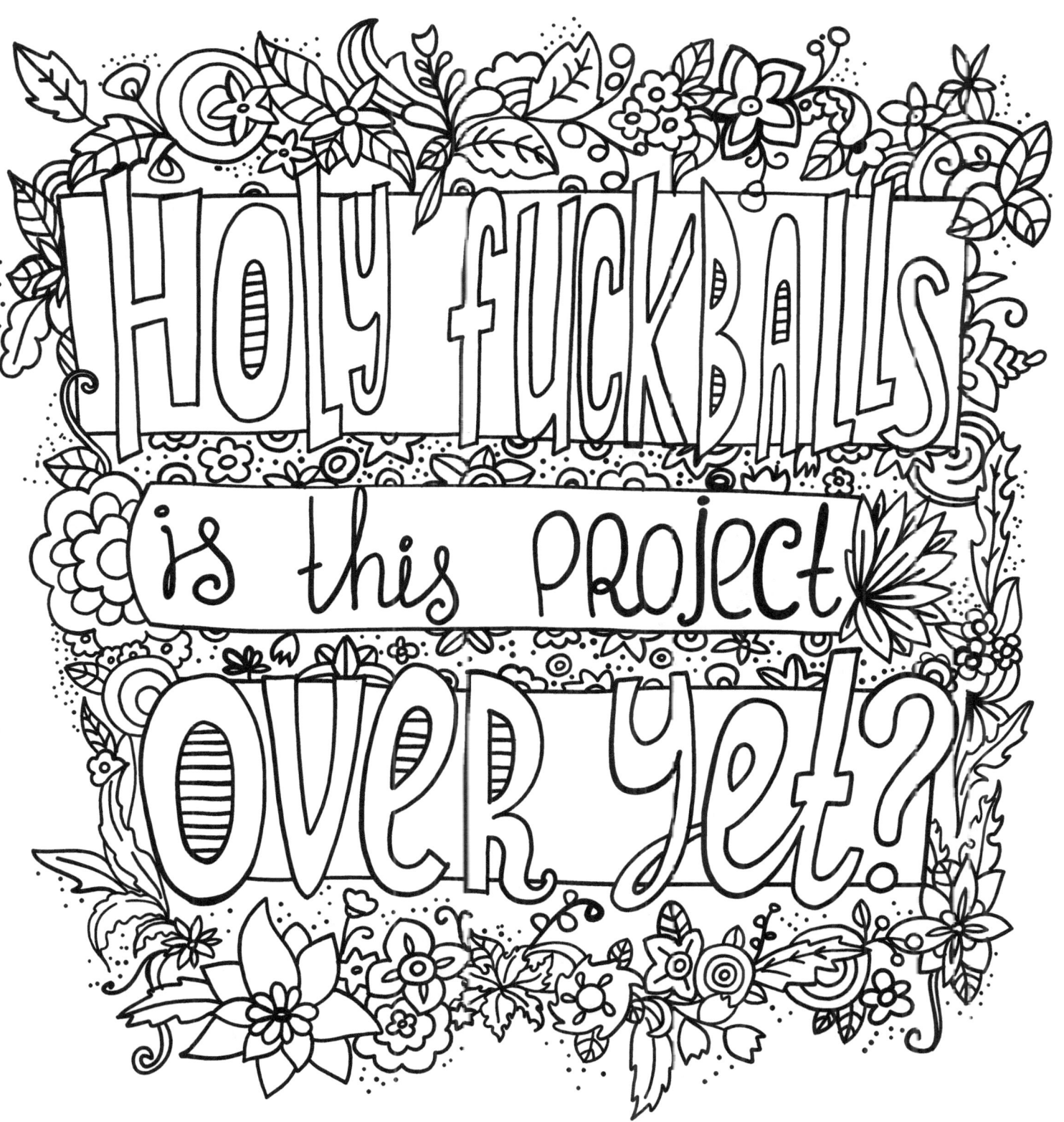

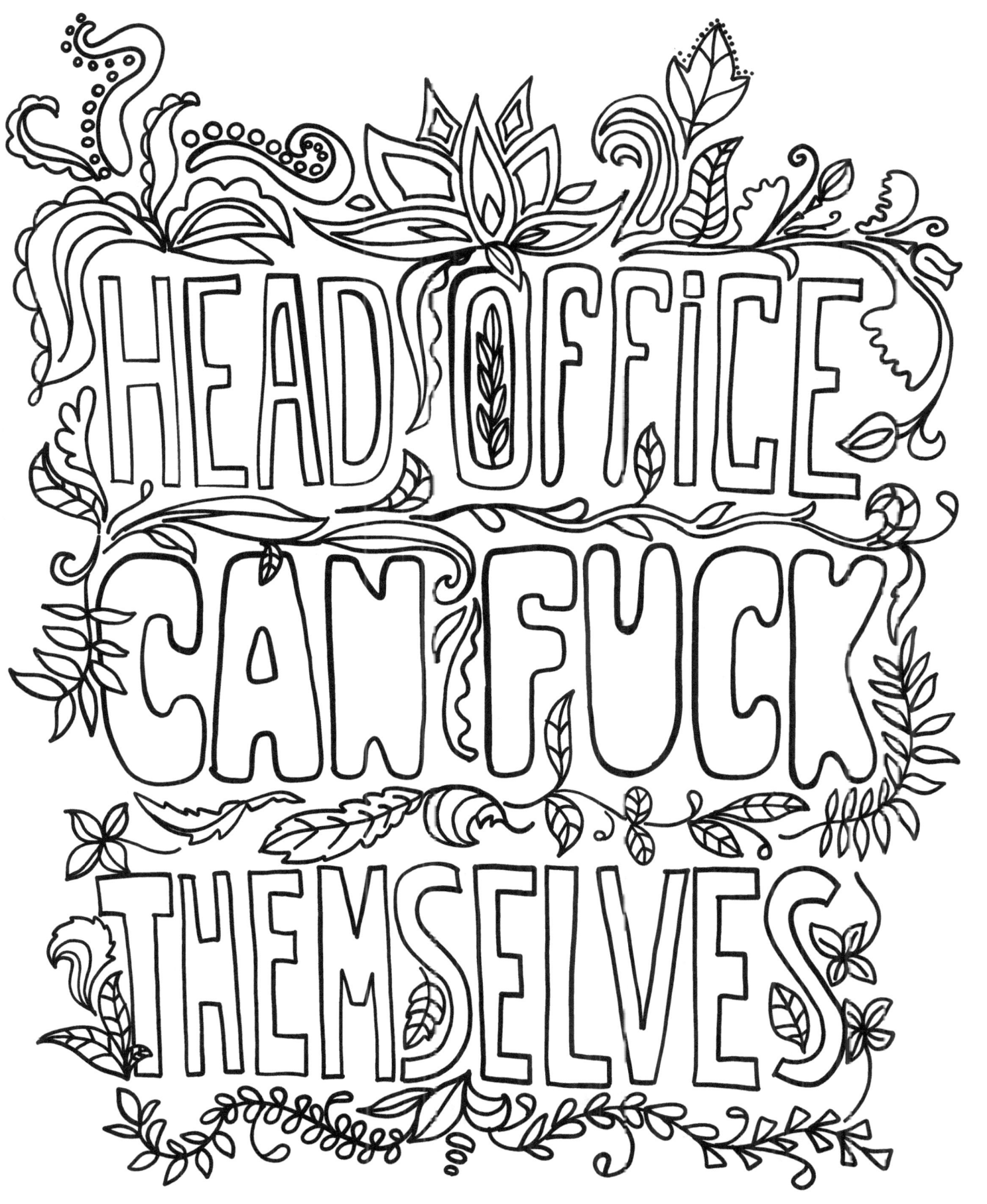

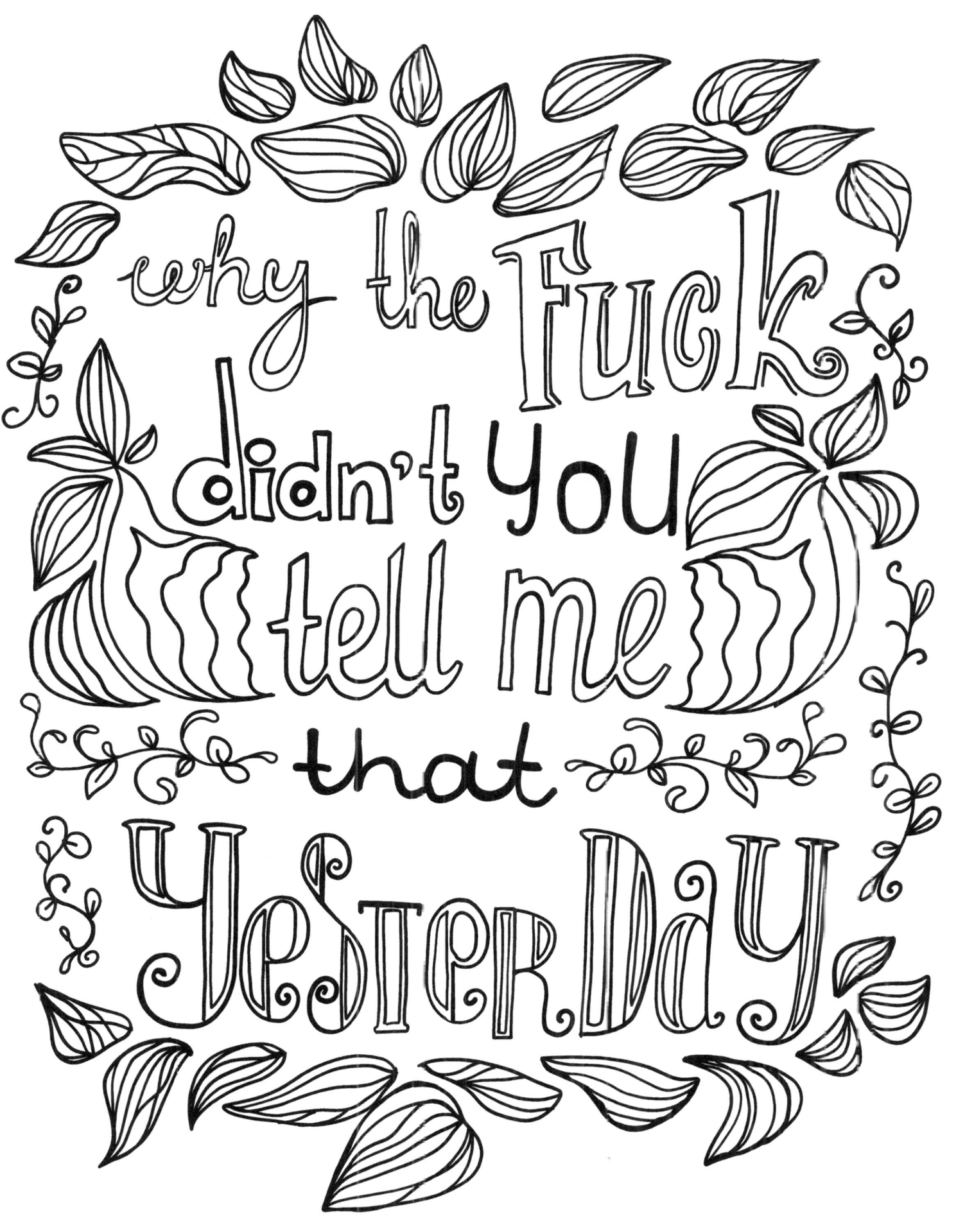

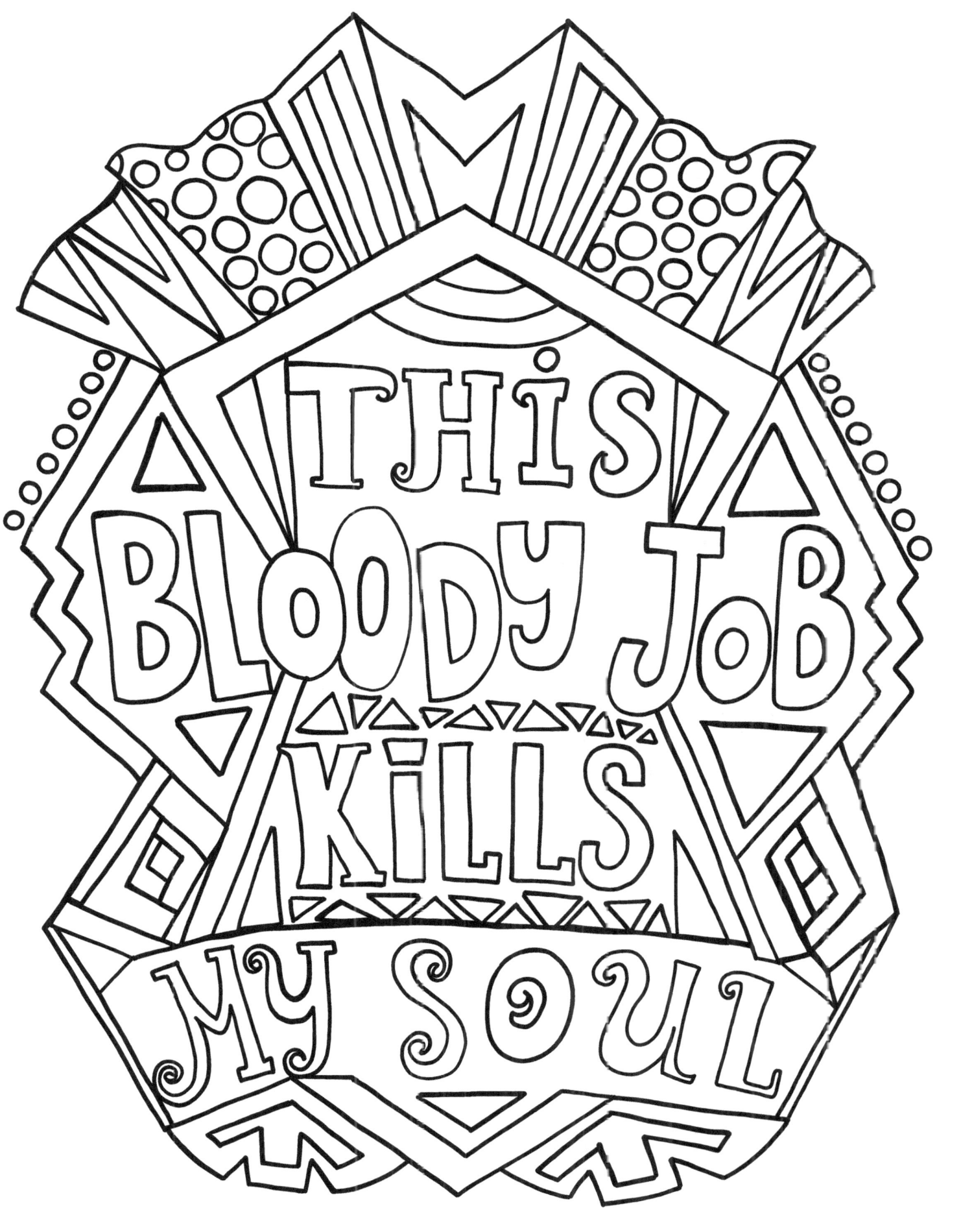

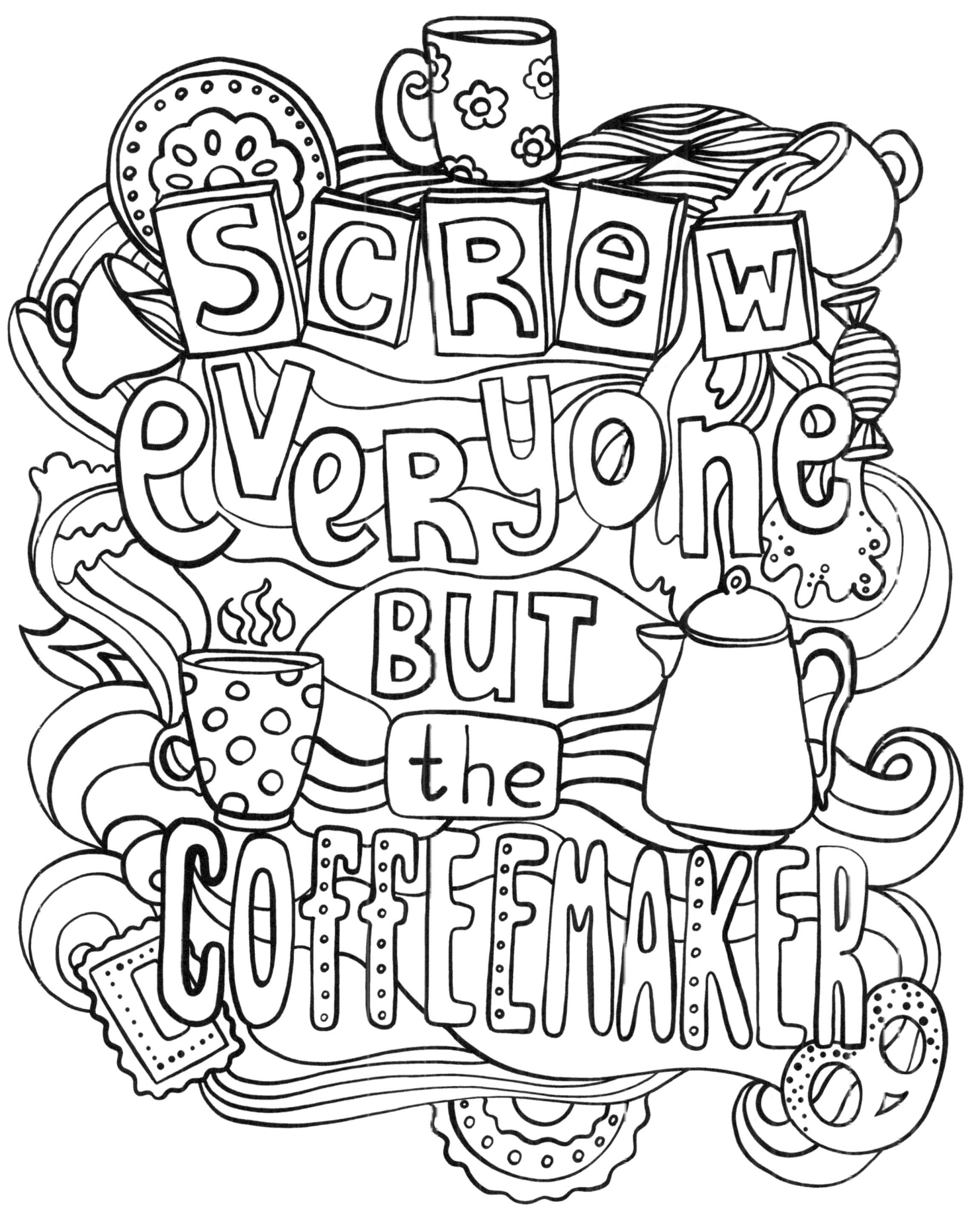

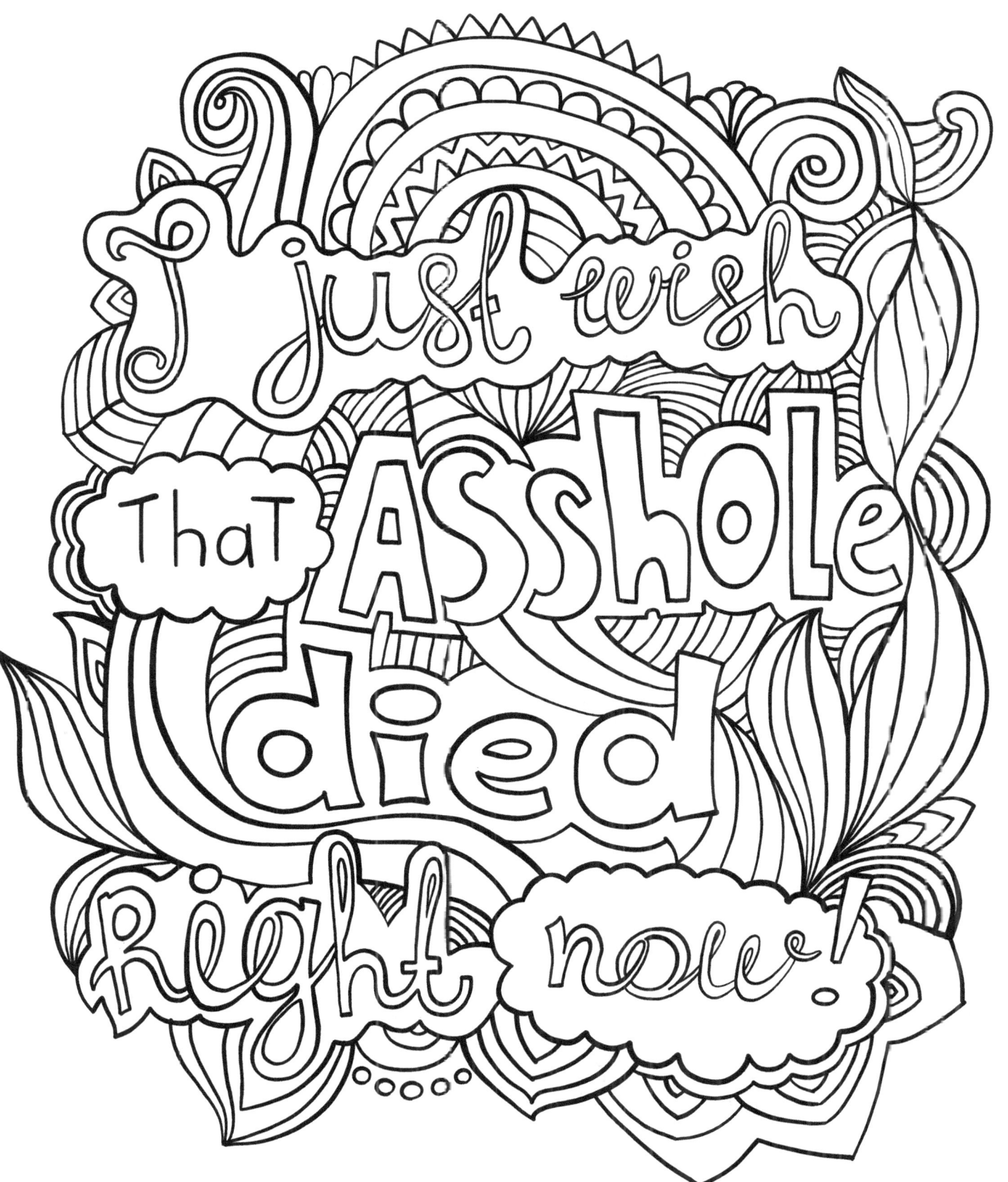

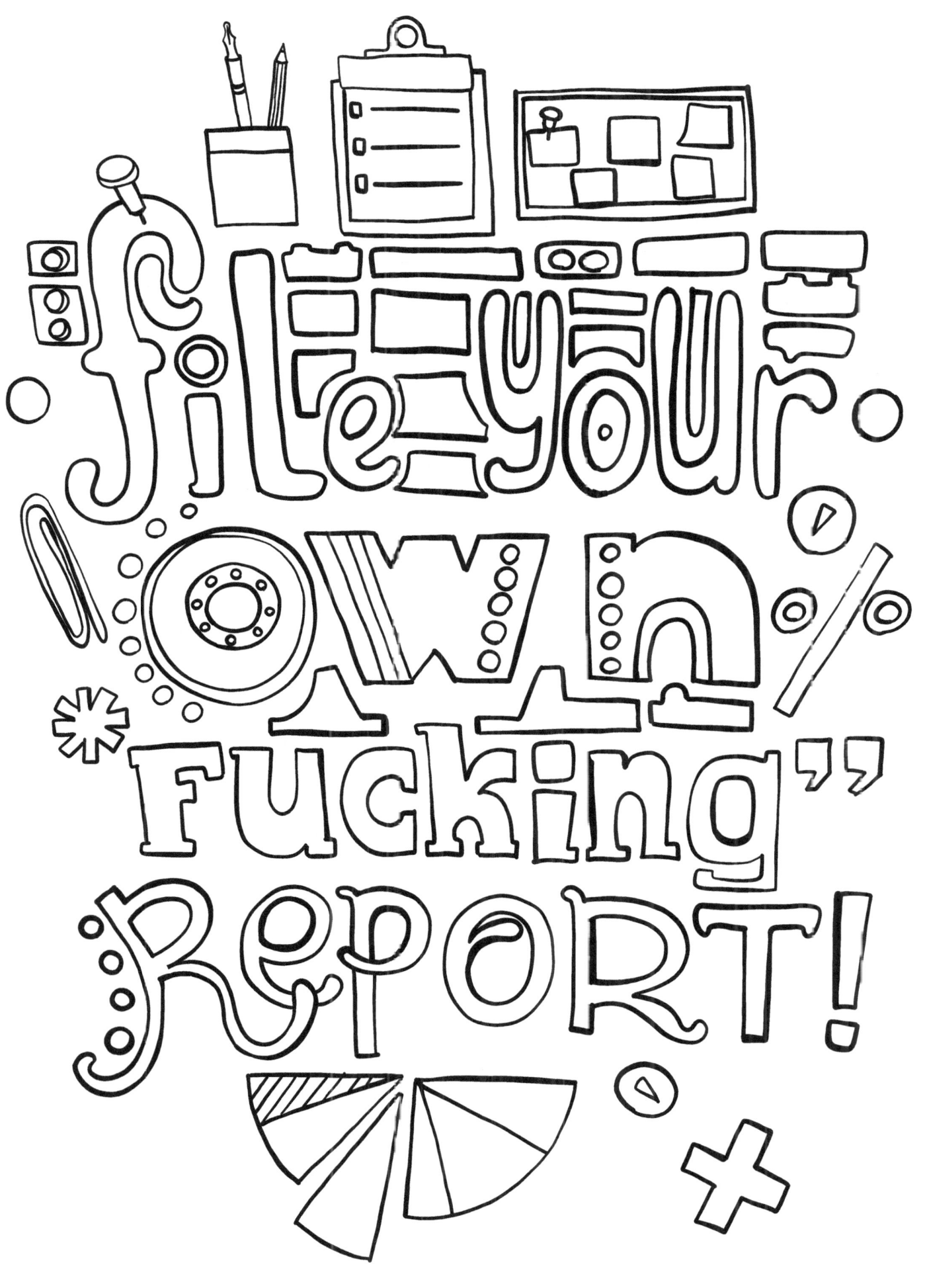

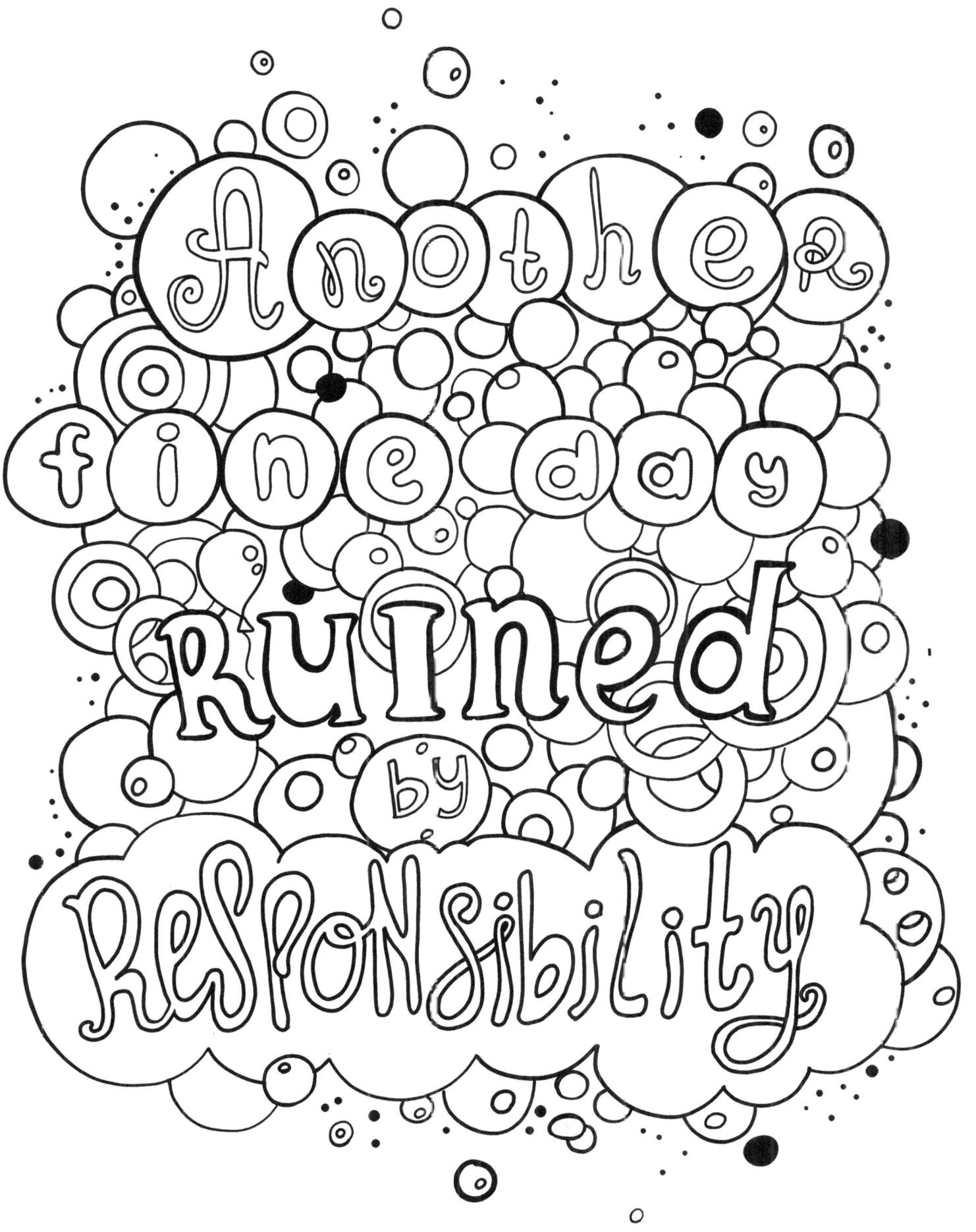

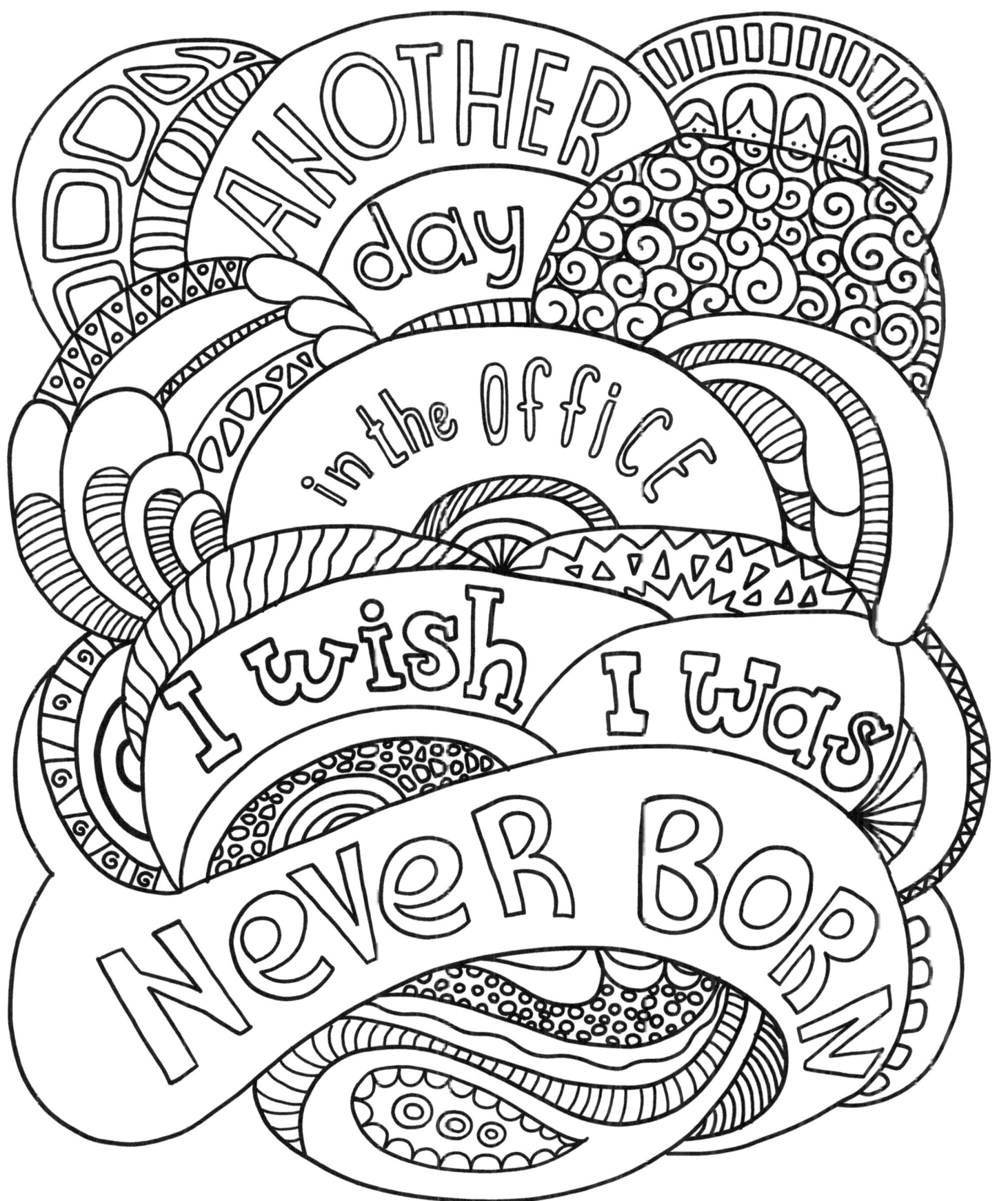

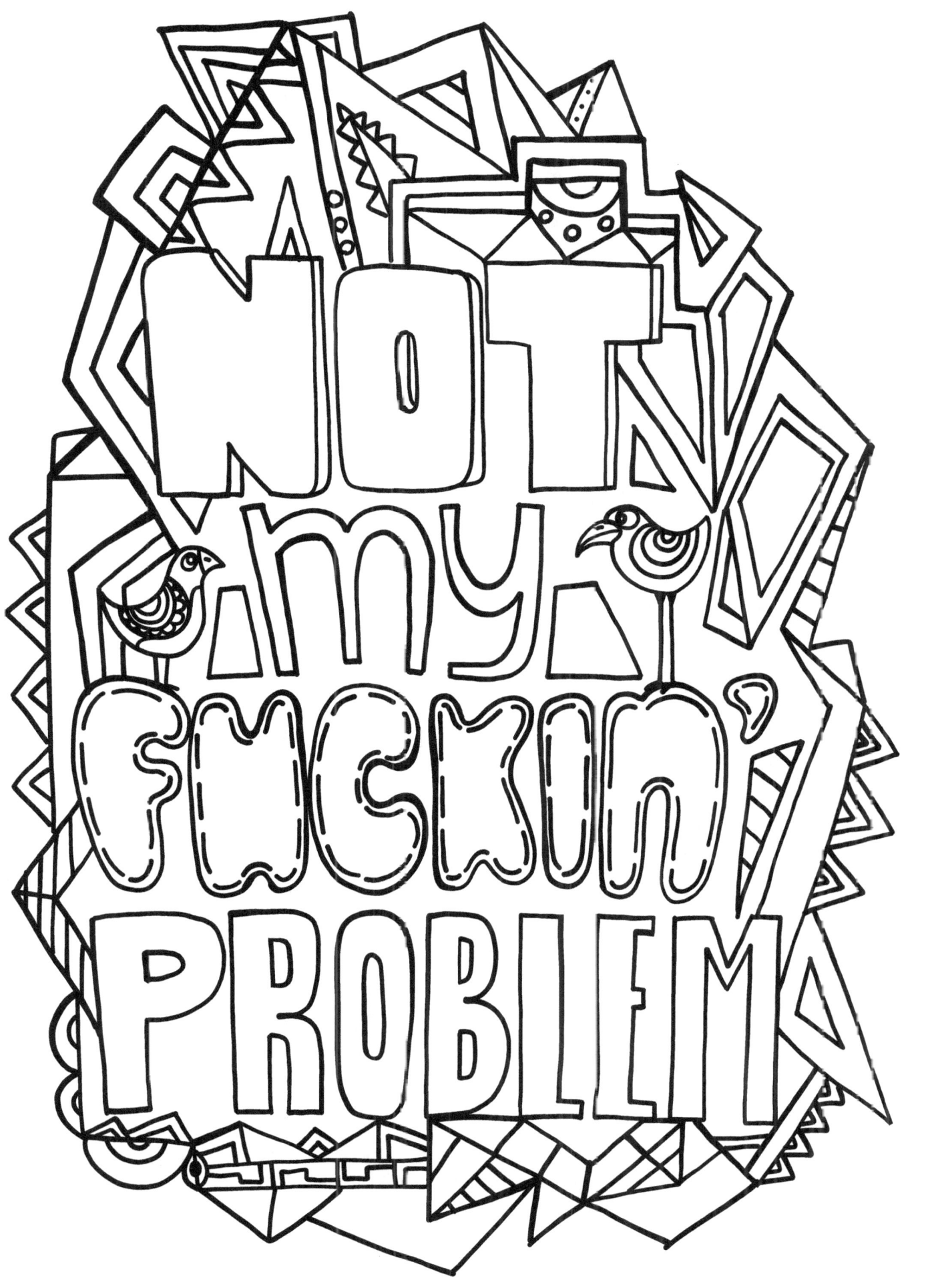

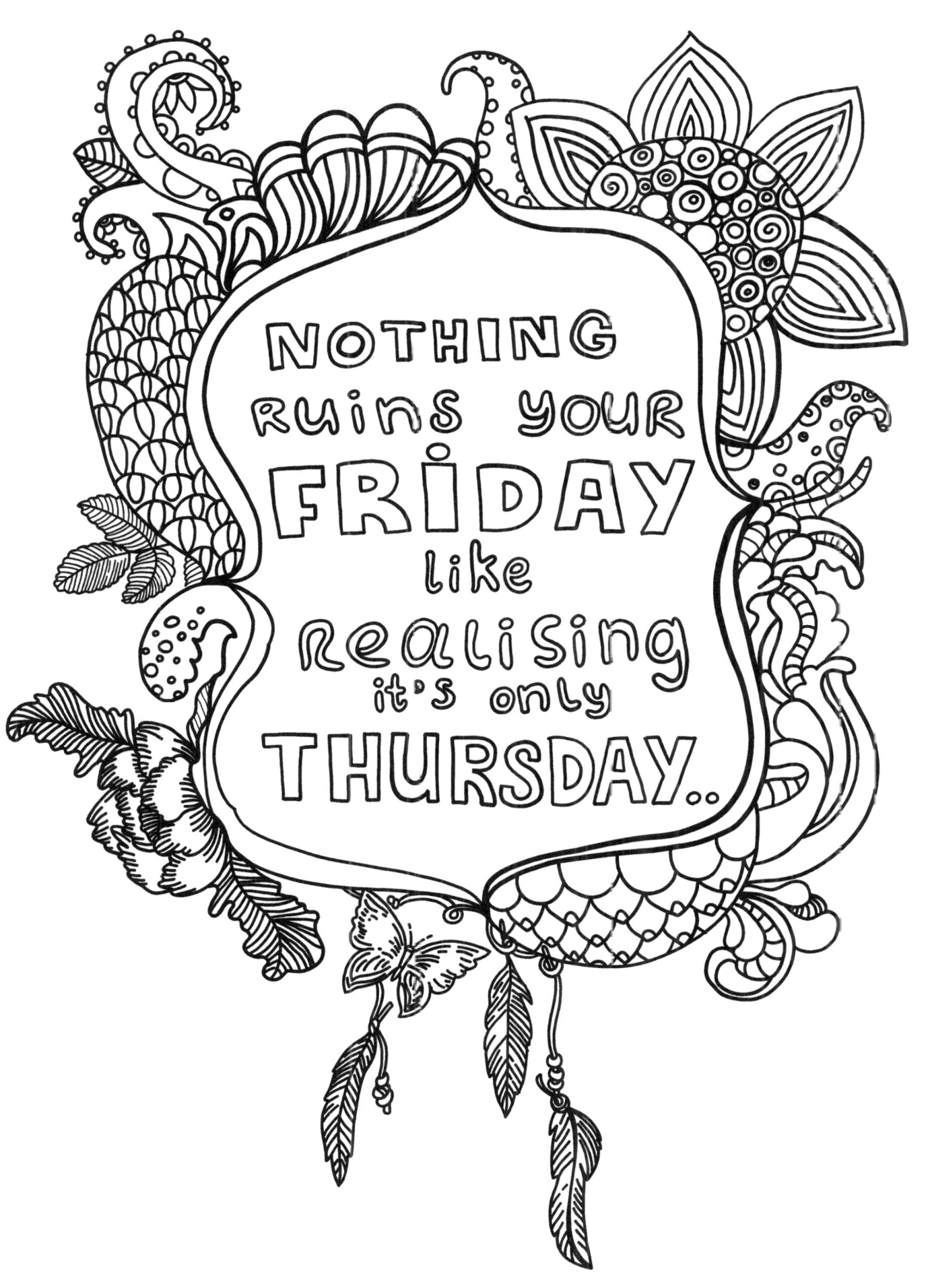

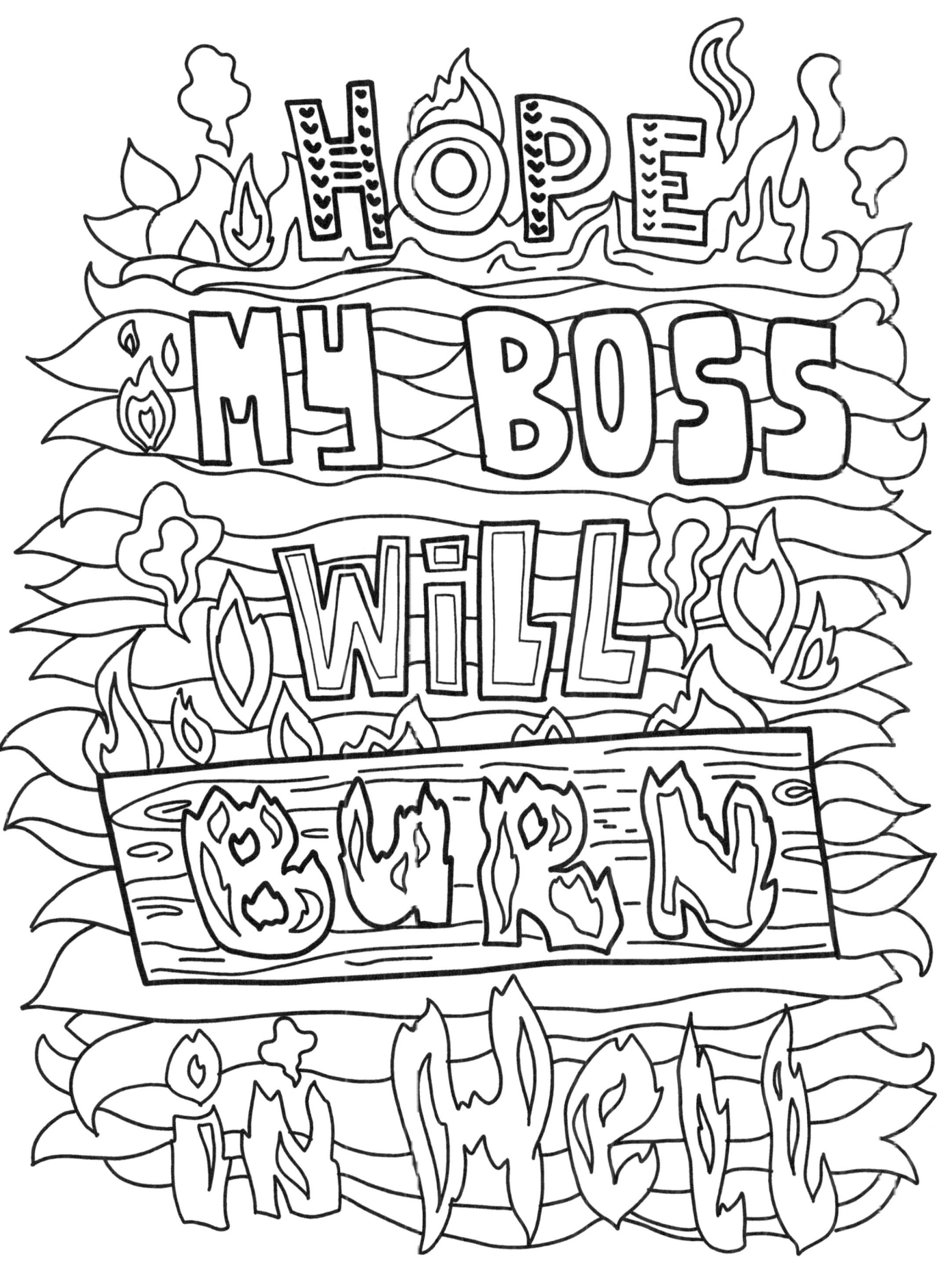

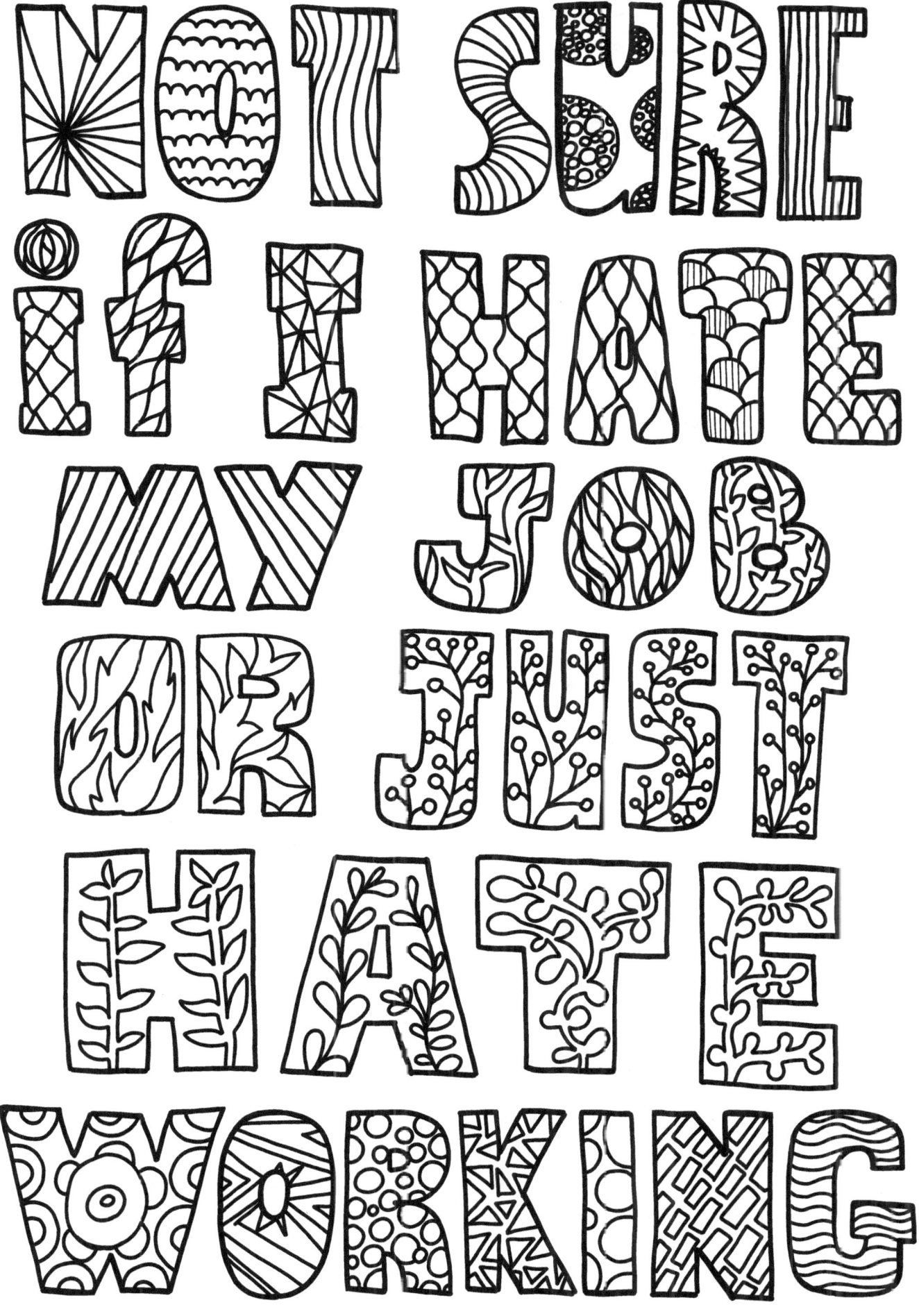

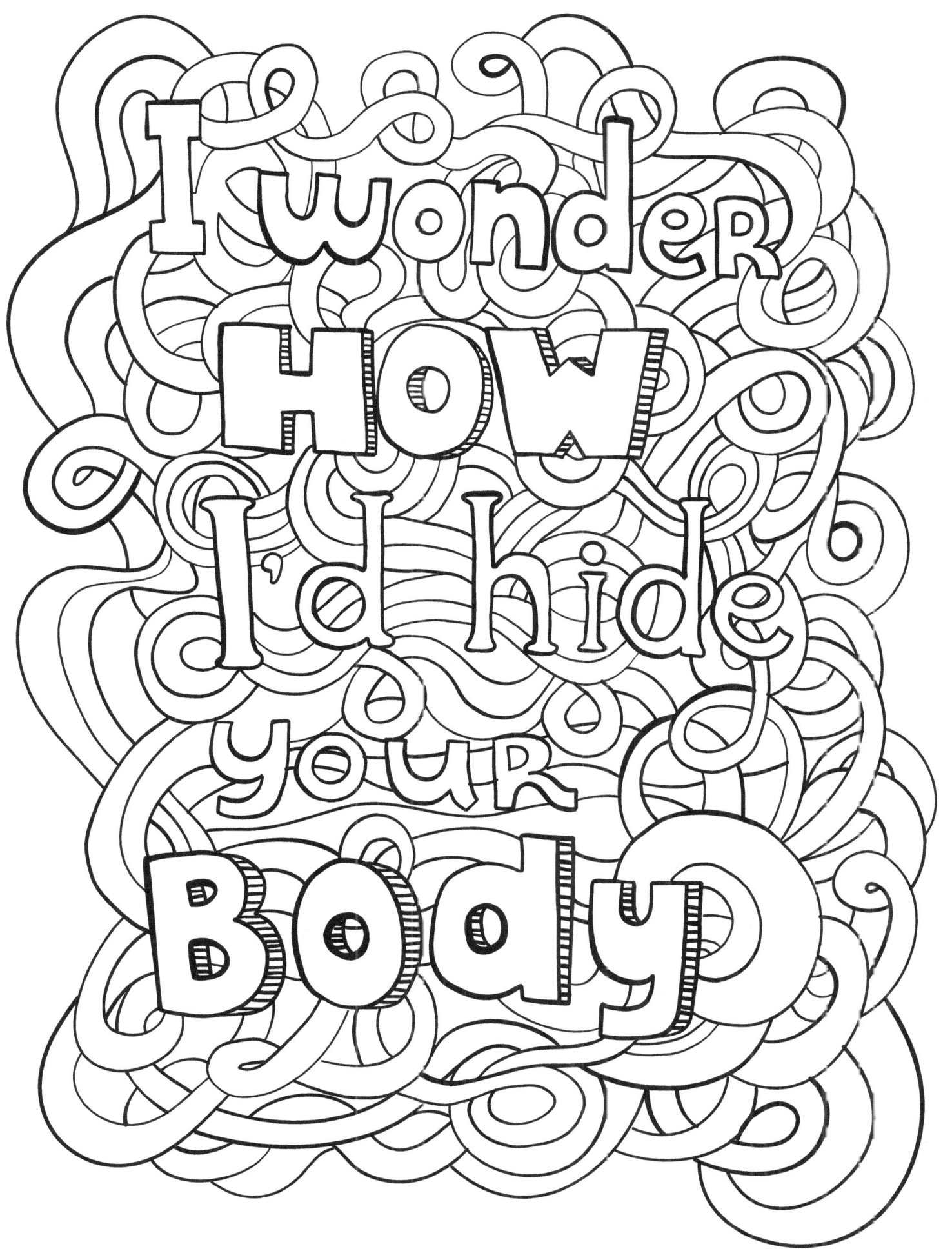

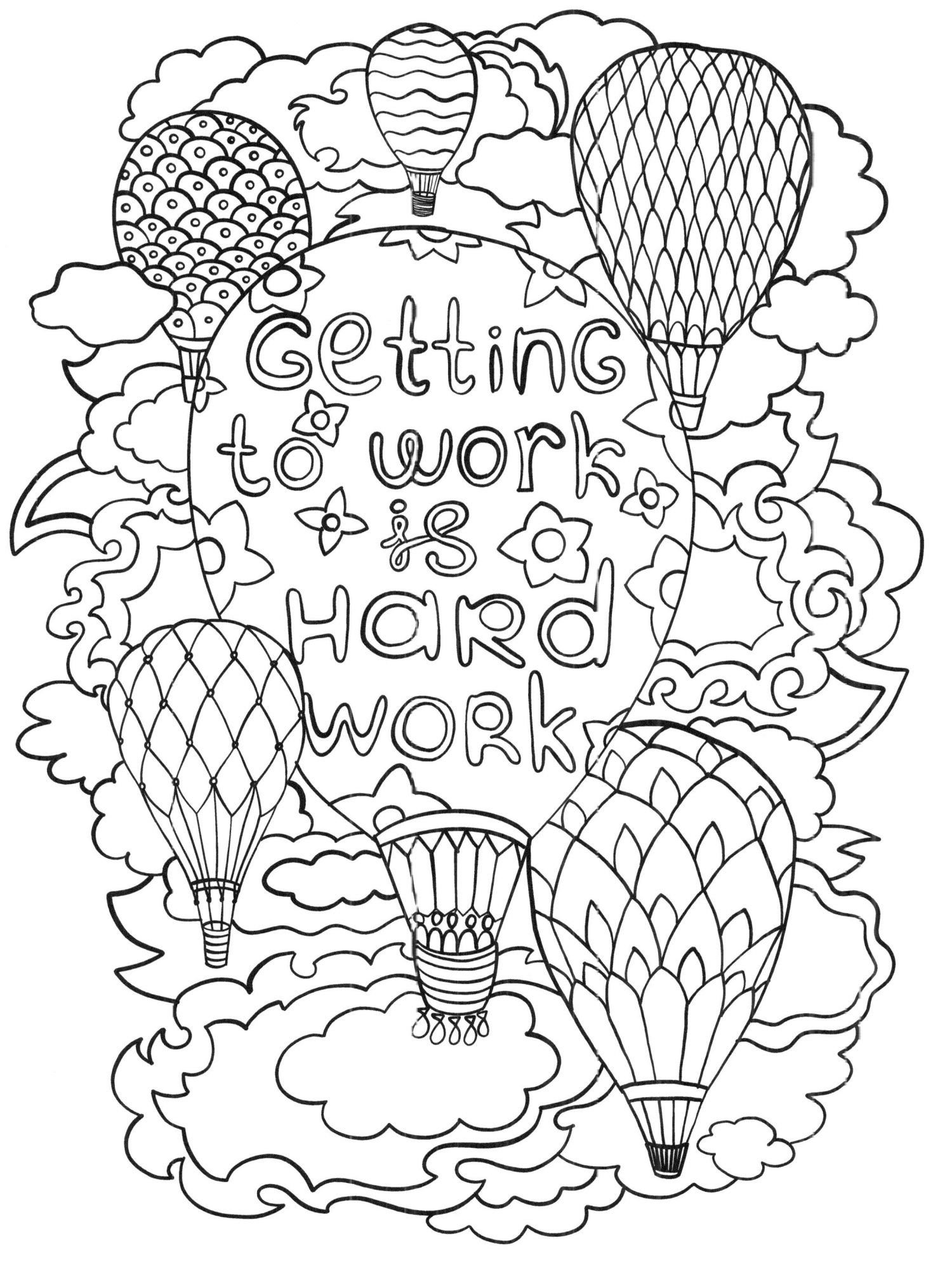

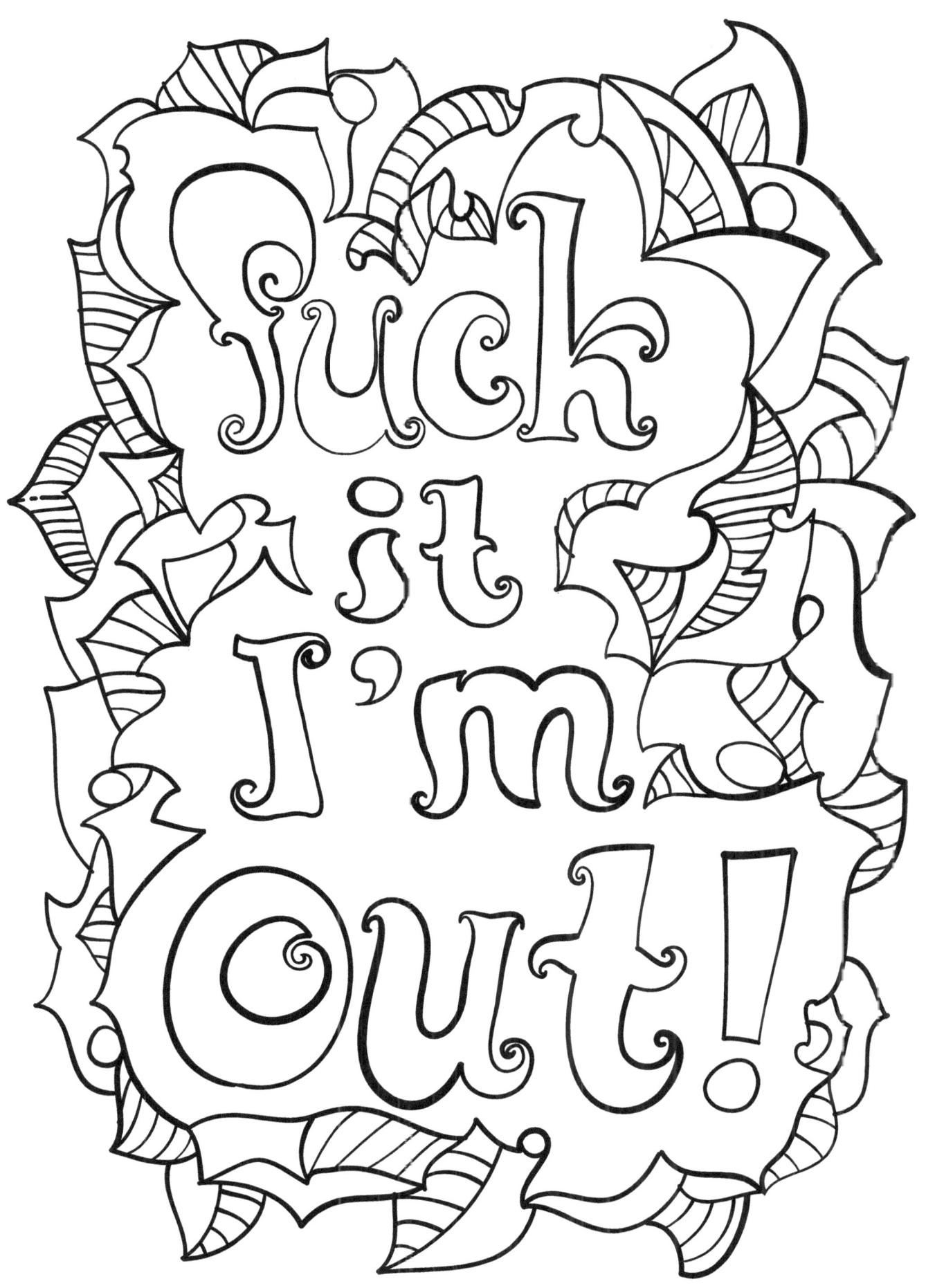

Thank you!

Dear creative,

Thank you so much for purchasing my book! I hope you had some fun coloring it.

All the illustrations are 100% original made by illustrator Evgeniya Pautova and are a subject of copyright.

Please, don't copy or reproduce any part of the book.

If you enjoyed the book feel free to share your experience and leave a review on Amazon. If would mean the world to me! Also it would motivate me to make more coloring books for you. :)

Let's help more people to get relaxed and relieve the stress together!

My contacts:
Website: https://wowyellow.com/
E-mail: jen@wowyellow.com
Any feedback is welcome.

Please share your results with me on Instagram: @wow-yellow_art. I'm super curious to see what you create!

Use the hashtag: **#wowyellowcolor** for your colored pieces so the world could see them. :) Thank you again!

Love,
Jen

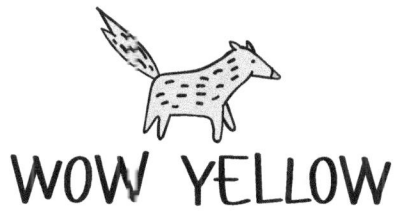

WOW YELLOW

www.ingramcontent.com/pod-product-compliance
Lightning Source LLC
Chambersburg PA
CBHW082316220526
45472CB00011B/1978